Extraordinary
BUGS

First published in paperback in 2013 by Wayland
Copyright © Wayland 2013

Wayland
338 Euston Road
London NW1 3BH

Wayland Australia
Level 17/207 Kent Street
Sydney, NSW 2000

Produced for Wayland by Calcium: www.calciumcreative.co.uk
Design: Simon Borrough
Editor: Sarah Eason
Picture researcher: Susannah Jayes
Commissioning Editor for Wayland: Victoria Brooker

Picture Acknowledgments: Alamy: Mark Bowler Amazon Images 22,
Nic Can Oudtshoorn 38, Ignacio Palacios 16; Flickr: Marschal Hedin 36; FLPA: 29
Gianpiero Ferrari; NHPA/Photoshot: George Bernard 19; Photolibrary: 4tr, 8, 12, 27,
37; Shutterstock: Evgeniy Ayupov 32, Stéphane Bidouze 9, Efendy 4cr, 10, Lukáš
Hejtman 33, Eric Isselée 15, 17, Sebastian Kaulitzki 43, Pawel Kielpinski 18, James
Laurie 5tr, 28, Roger De Marfa 23, Rodney Mehring 25, Dmitrijs Mihejevs14,
Orionmystery/Flickr 5bl & br, 6, 13, 40, Photofish 7, Graham Prentice 35,
Dr. Morley Read 26, 42, p.schwarz 4bl 21, Smit 33, Carolina K. Smith, M.D. 31,
Ian Tragen 19, Birute Vijeikiene 30, Wattana 41, Fong Kam Yee 39; Wikipedia:
Axel Strauß 11, Hans Hillewaert 24.

Wayland
British Library Cataloguing in Publication Data
Gray, Leon, 1974-
   Extraordinary bugs.
   1. Insects--Juvenile literature.
   I. Title
   595.7-dc22

ISBN: 978 0 7502 7162 2

Printed in China
Wayland is a division of Hachette Children's Books,
an Hachette UK company.

www.hachette.co.uk

Contents

Amazing bugs

The world is full of bizarre and beastly creepy crawlies of all different shapes and sizes. Most of them, such as the brilliant blue damselfly and the magnificent monarch butterfly, are harmless creatures that add a splash of colour to the world. Others, such as the tiny mosquito, may look dull and harmless but actually kill millions of people every year, by spreading deadly diseases such as **malaria**.

In this book you will meet some of the world's most unusual insects and **arachnids**, from exploding beetles and long-nosed weevils to **microscopic** mites and monstrous spiders. Some minibeasts don't just look odd, they feed in weird ways, too.

Thorn bug

Dung beetle

For example, the maggots of the gruesome botfly devour human flesh, and the strange scarab beetle survives by eating animal poo. And then there are the creepy crawlies that are simply too unusual to explain, such as the spider that looks and smells like bird poo, or the flies that lay their eggs inside the bodies of ants – and make their heads fall off!

Robber fly

4

Insect groups

Scientists like to organize insects into groups, so that's what we've done in this book, too. Most creepy crawlies are insects. All insects have six legs and three main body parts – a head, a middle part called the **thorax** and an end part called the **abdomen**. Almost all insects **hatch** from an egg and go through a number of changes to become adults.

Monarch butterfly

Scientists think there are more than 8 million different types of insect. They organize similar insects into smaller groups. So there is one group of insects called beetles and another group called butterflies and moths.

Another group of creepy crawlies is the arachnids. They include minibeasts such as spiders and scorpions. All arachnids have eight legs and two main body parts. Unlike insects, arachnids do not change to become adults. Instead, they shed their skin every so often to grow, in a process called **moulting**.

Blister beetle

Assassin bug

Assassin bug

There are thousands of different kinds of assassin bug. They all eat other animals, including humans. When assassin bugs bite, they inject their **prey** with their deadly **saliva**. The saliva contains substances that turn the insides of the prey into a liquid. The assassin bug then sucks up the juices. Tiny, sticky hairs cover the legs of some assassin bugs. The bugs use them to hold the prey as they eat it.

Kissing bugs

Some blood-sucking assassin bugs are known as 'kissing bugs' because they bite people in their sleep, especially on soft body parts such as the lips.

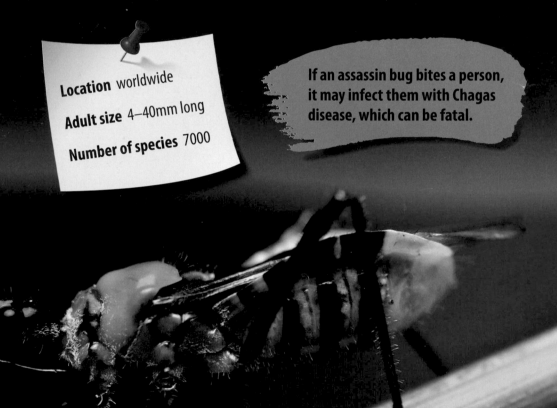

Location worldwide

Adult size 4–40mm long

Number of species 7000

If an assassin bug bites a person, it may infect them with Chagas disease, which can be fatal.

Giant water bug

Location worldwide, especially the Americas and East Asia

Adult size up to about 12cm long

Number of species 100

Eggs

The female giant water bug lays more than 100 eggs on the male's back. He looks after them for three weeks before they hatch.

FREAKY FEATURE

Substances in the saliva of the giant water bug turn human flesh into a liquid once it has been bitten.

Giant water bugs are large, deadly **predators** with a painful bite. Most **species** lie on the bottom of rivers and ponds, waiting for passing insects, small fish and frogs. When the prey gets within range, the water bug strikes.

Eating the biter

In some countries, such as Thailand and other parts of South-east Asia, people eat giant water bugs. But the people who catch them must watch out! Giant water bugs play dead when they are caught – but then suddenly come back to life!

7

Thorn bug

The thorn bug gets its name from the thorny growth on the middle of its body, or thorax. This growth looks like the sharp thorn of a plant. It gives the bugs **camouflage**, and also stops predators, such as birds, from eating them.

Location North and South America

Adult size around 1cm long

Number of species more than 3000

Sap feeders

Thorn bugs eat **sap** – the juices that run through the stems of plants. They use their sharp mouthparts to bite into the stems and suck up the sap. Female thorn bugs lay their eggs inside the stems of plants, so that the insect **larvae** can get food as soon as they hatch.

The thorn-like growth of each thorn bug can vary greatly in size, shape and colour.

Cicada

Location worldwide

Adult size largest species up to 15cm long

Number of species 2500

Cicadas are well known because they 'sing' loudly. To make this noise, they **vibrate** parts of their body. Cicada songs are often heard on hot summer days, when the males 'sing' to attract females to **mate**.

Life cycle

After mating, female cicadas lay their eggs inside the twigs and branches of trees. When the eggs hatch, the larvae fall to the ground and **burrow** into the soil. All the adults then emerge at the same time, to mate and so continue the **life cycle**. The larvae of some species in North America can stay in the soil for up to 17 years.

Cicadas have large eyes and see-through wings with prominent dark veins.

CICADA FOOD

In some parts of the world, people eat cicadas. They prefer to eat the females because they are bigger than the males.

Dung beetle

Location worldwide except Antarctica

Adult size 1mm–6cm long

Number of species more than 5000

As their name suggests, **dung** beetles eat animal poo. This may seem disgusting, but the dung beetle does an important job by cleaning the soil. Some dung beetles roll the dung into balls, which they keep as a food store. Others bury it in underground 'storerooms'. A few species actually live in the animal poo! Scientists working in Africa once found 16,000 dung beetles in 1.5 kilograms of elephant poo. All dung beetles prefer to eat the dung that is produced by animals that eat plants. They use their amazing **sense** of smell to find the poo.

Ancient Egypt

The ancient Egyptians worshipped a kind of dung beetle called a scarab. They believed that these beetles made the Sun rise every morning. The dung balls they rolled were a **symbol** of the Sun as it 'rolled' across the sky during the day.

SCARAB JEWELLERY

The scarab beetle was so important to the ancient Egyptians that they included it in their pictures and crafts, such as jewellery.

Dung beetles can roll balls of dung up to 50 times their own weight. They often fight each other over these smelly food stores!

Giraffe weevil

Location Madagascar

Adult size up to 8cm long

Number of species 1

FREAKY FEATURE

The neck of the giraffe beetle can he up to three times the length of its body!

The incredibly long neck of the male giraffe weevil gives this beetle its common name.

The giraffe weevil lives in the warm **rainforests** of Madagascar – an island off the east coast of Africa. Just like a giraffe, the neck of the male giraffe weevil is very long, much longer than the female's. The males use their long necks to build nests, by rolling leaves into tube shapes. Females mate with the males that have built the best nests. Then they lay their eggs in the middle of the tube.

Giant snout

Another insect called a giraffe beetle lives in New Zealand. Like their relatives in Madagascar, male giraffe beetles are long, but it is the **snout** that makes up most of their length – almost half the length of their body.

Bombardier beetle

Bombardier beetles take their name from the way they protect themselves from predators. These beetles 'bombard' their enemies with a boiling mixture of poisonous substances. They release the substances from **sacs** near the rear end of their bodies. When the substances mix they explode, and the explosion forces the poisonous liquid out of the beetle's body with a loud pop. The substances are strong enough to kill predators such as ants, and they can even burn human skin.

Location worldwide except Antarctica and Asia

Adult size 5–13mm long

Number of species 500

FREAKY FEATURE
The beetle can swivel its body to shoot the spray with amazing accuracy.

Bang! The bombardier beetle explodes, and a mixture of boiling poisons shoots out over this person's finger.

Blister beetle

Location worldwide, except Antarctica

Adult size up to 4cm long

Number of species about 7500

The orange head of this blister beetle warns other animals to stay away – or suffer the painful consequences.

As their name suggests, **blister** beetles release a substance that causes **blisters** on human skin. The chemical is in the beetle's saliva and it uses it for defence. When it bites another animal it gives it blisters. The chemical is also in its blood, so squashing a beetle or eating it also causes blisters, as blood seeps out of the beetle's body. Many blister beetles are brightly coloured.

Horse killer

The blisters these beetles cause are painful to people, but they are not deadly. Other animals, such as horses, can die after eating beetles that live in their food.

HELPFUL HEALERS

Doctors used to use the chemical released by blister beetles to remove **warts** on people's skin.

13

Goliath beetle

Location central Africa

Adult size males up to 11cm long

Number of species 5

Goliath beetles are the true heavyweights of the insect world. The larvae grow up to an enormous 13 centimetres long, and can weigh up to 100 grams. They grow so big by eating rotting plants in the soil. It takes about four months for the larvae to grow to their full size. Then they bury themselves in the soil and change into adult beetles.

Adult Goliath beetles feast on ripe fruit and sugary plant sap. This food is full of energy.

Adult life

Adult males are bigger than females. The biggest males can be up to 11 centimetres long and weigh about 50 grams. Males have large horns on their heads, which they use in fights with each other for the females. Female beetles have wedge-shaped heads. This helps them dig the holes in which they bury their eggs.

WHAT'S IN A NAME?

The Goliath beetle is named after the mythical giant Goliath, who was killed by a boy called David.

14

Hercules beetle

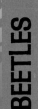

The Hercules beetle takes its name from the Greek hero Hercules, who was famous for being very strong. There are six species, and they live in the **tropical** rainforests of Central and South America. These giant beetles are one of the world's largest insects, but the males are much bigger than the females because they have huge horns that make up most of their length. They use these horns in fights over females – the winner is the beetle that can flip its opponent onto its back.

The male Hercules beetle uses its horns in fights over food – as well as females!

Location Central and South America

Adult size males up to 17cm long

Number of species 6

Super strong

The Hercules beetle is one of the world's strongest animals. It can carry up to 850 times its own body weight – that's about the same as an average adult person carrying six elephants!

15

Borneo stick insect

The Borneo stick insect is the world's longest insect. Stick insects are masters of disguise. They have slender brown and green bodies that look like the green shoots and twigs of plants. Stick insects gently swing from side to side, to copy plants as they sway in the breeze.

Location Borneo

Adult size up to 56.7cm long

Number of species 3000

PET CORNER
Many people keep stick insects as pets. They are easy to look after, but take care when you pick them up — they can bite!

Now you see me... the body of the Borneo stick insect camouflages it among the leaves of its rainforest habitat.

Borneo stick insects live high up in the trees. Females lay eggs with wing-like parts that help the eggs glide from tree to tree. In this way, the eggs spread through the rainforest.

Record breaker

Scientists found the world's longest stick insect in the rainforest of Borneo in 2008. It is 56.7cm long and is on display at the Natural History Museum in London.

Leaf insect

Most leaf insects live in the tropical rainforests of South-east Asia and Australia. These amazing insects are closely related to stick insects, and look almost exactly like the leaves of a plant. They have dull green and brown bodies, to blend in with the plants where they live. Some even have blotches, spots and bite marks on their bodies to copy the marks on real leaves. They use their disguise to hide from predators.

Location Asia and Australia

Adult size about 10cm long

Number of species about 30

Mating games

Male leaf insects are smaller than females. They fly around the treetops, searching for a female to mate with. Leaf insects sway from side to side as they move, so it looks as if they are swaying in the breeze.

FREAKY FEATURE

The females of some leaf insects can also lay eggs without mating with males. When their eggs hatch, all the young will be females.

Leaf or insect?! The insect's clever disguise ensures that predators find it almost impossible to tell the difference.

17

Orchid mantis

The orchid mantis lives in the tropical rainforests of South-east Asia. It uses camouflage to hide in flowers – from both predators and prey. It is an unusual shape, and coloured to match the flowers of plants such as orchids and papaya trees. Its legs look like the petals of the flowers. Every so often, the orchid mantis sheds its skin, or moults, to grow bigger. With each moult, its colours develop to blend in with its surroundings.

Hunting

The orchid mantis is a fearsome predator that hunts during the day. It lies in wait for any unsuspecting prey to pass by. It usually eats fruit flies and other small insects, but it will gobble up almost anything it can catch, including small lizards.

The pink and white body of this orchid mantis matches the flowers of the plants on which it lives.

FREAKY FEATURE

When threatened, the orchid mantis is vicious and bites out at everything within reach.

Location South-east Asia

Adult size up to 7.5cm long

Number of species 1

Praying mantis

The name praying mantis refers to one species, the European mantis from southern Europe. This insect ranges in colour from bright green to brown. The praying mantis takes its name from the prayer-like position it has when it lies in wait for passing prey. The praying mantis has a triangle-shaped head, which it can turn through a complete half circle to spot a meal. It eats mainly insects and other small animals.

Location Central and South America

Adult size males up to 17cm long

Number of species 6

FREAKY FEATURE

The mantis's front legs have rows of sharp spines that it uses to hold onto its prey, before eating it head first!

Food for thought

One of the oddest habits of the praying mantis is **cannibalism**. Females are usually much bigger than males, and they often eat their partners after mating! No one really knows why this happens. The best explanation is that it gives the females a meal when they need energy to make sure their babies survive.

Praying mantids prey on animals such as frogs, small lizards and even rodents such as mice.

Ant decapitating fly

The female ant **decapitating** fly is a gruesome creature. She lays her eggs inside the bodies of ants. When the eggs hatch, the maggots eat the insides of the ant, including its brain. With no brain, the ant wanders around like a zombie. Eventually, the maggot releases a substance that make the ant's head fall off. The maggot then transforms into the adult fly, and emerges from the dead ant.

Safety in numbers

No ant really wants to be eaten from the inside out, so the ants march in pairs to protect themselves from attack – with one ant acting as a lookout for the flies.

An ant decapitating fly hovers around a group of ants, waiting to dart down and lay her eggs inside the body of a victim.

Location South America

Adult size a few millimetres long

Number of species 110

FREAKY FEATURE

An ant can survive with no brain because other nerves take control of its body.

Robber fly

As flies go, there is nothing very unusual about the appearance of the robber fly. It has two large **compound eyes** on each side of its head, with three simple **eyespots** between them. This gives the fly excellent eyesight.

Location worldwide

Adult size 3–5mm long

Number of species more than 7000

Feeding habits

But robber flies are deadly predators that hunt other insects and spiders. When the fly attacks, it stabs its victim with its long, tube-like mouthparts. The robber fly injects its prey with substances that turn it into liquid food. It then sucks up its meal.

FREAKY FEATURE

Some robber flies have fat bodies with black and yellow stripes to copy the markings of bumblebees. This helps to stop predators from attacking them.

The thick bristles around the robber fly's face protect it from prey that put up a fight!

21

Human botfly

There are about 40 different types of botfly, but only one species lays its eggs inside people. Human skin is tough, so the human botfly needs help to get its eggs inside. Mosquitoes are perfect for this, because they feed on human blood.

Flesh feeder

First, the botflies lay their eggs on mosquitoes. Then the mosquitoes use their sharp, piercing mouthparts to break through the skin. As the mosquito takes a bite, heat from the person's body makes the botfly eggs hatch. The botfly maggots then burrow into the skin and start to eat human flesh. The maggots can survive for eight weeks inside the human, before they burrow out and change into flies.

Location Central America

Adult size 12–19mm long

Number of species 40

BOTFLY REMOVAL
It is easy to remove botfly maggots. You smear the hole with petroleum jelly. This suffocates them. You can then squeeze them out once they're dead!

The human botfly maggot uses its drill-shaped head to burrow a tunnel through human flesh.

Mosquito

Mosquitoes are small flies with a big reputation. They carry tiny **parasites** that cause one of the world's deadliest diseases – malaria. Only a few different types of mosquito carry the parasites that cause malaria. They live in tropical regions in Central and South America, Africa and Asia. Mosquitoes pass on the parasites to people when they bite them. The females carry the parasites in their saliva. When they bite, they inject some of the saliva into the blood. The parasites then infect the body.

FREAKY FEATURE

Mosquitoes find people by detecting the **carbon dioxide** we breathe out. They can also sense our heat and sweat.

Deadly disease

Millions of people die every year from malaria. Mosquitoes usually bite people who are asleep. Sleeping under mosquito nets is one of the best ways to stop the spread of this deadly disease.

Location worldwide

Adult size up to 16mm long

Number of species 3500

A female mosquito sinks her mouthparts into the skin to suck up a meal of human blood.

23

Bullet ant

Bullet ants live in the tropical rainforests of Central and South America. They gather in large colonies at the base of trees, and will attack anything that wanders close by, including people. Bullet ants may be tiny, but they pack a powerful punch.

Location Central and South America

Adult size 2.5cm long

Number of species 1

The sting of the bullet ant is more painful than that of any other ant, wasp or bee in the world.

Nasty sting

The sting of a bullet ant is so painful that some people have said it feels like being shot with a bullet – which explains their name. They are also called '24-hour ants' because the burning pain that follows a sting lasts for 24 hours.

COMING OF AGE

In some tribes that live in the Brazilian rainforest, a boy can only become a warrior if he can endure being stung by a bullet ant up to 20 times – without screaming!

Africanized honey bee

The Africanized honey bee is a cross between two different bees – the European honey bee and the African honey bee. It looks almost exactly the same as its European cousin, but it is much more aggressive. If you stumble upon a nest of Africanized honey bees, you had better watch out!

Killer bees

Africanized honey bees are known as killer bees. It is true that you can die by being stung by thousands of bees, but only a few people are killed every year. However, people are concerned because the bees are spreading into areas where lots of people live.

STRENGTH IN NUMBERS

What makes the Africanized honey bee so dangerous is that they swarm and attack intruders, including people, in such large numbers.

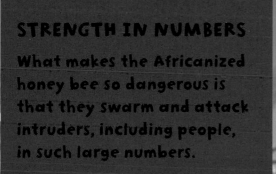

Location southern United States and Central and South America

Adult size up to 2cm long

Number of species 1

Africanized honey bees swarm around the branch of a tree. These bees will attack anything that disturbs their nest.

25

Army ant

Army ants are deadly predators that leave a trail of destruction behind them. They get their name because they move around in large 'armies', called swarm raids, looking for food. One swarm raid may contain 200,000 ants and be up to 14 metres wide!

Fearsome feeders

These large ants are some of the most feared insect predators. They have massive jaws, called mandibles, to cut up their prey into pieces. In some army ants, the mandibles are half the length of their whole body! Army ants will kill and eat almost anything that is unfortunate enough to wander into their path – usually insects and spiders, but sometimes small vertebrates (animals with a backbone).

Location Africa, Asia and South America

Adult size up to 1.5cm long

Number of species 20

An army ant guard has huge mandibles that it uses to defend other members of the **colony**.

FREAKY FEATURE
Army ants do not build **permanent** nests. Instead, they build a **temporary** nest by joining their bodies together!

Asian giant hornet

The Asian giant hornet is a large insect with a deadly sting in its tail. It has a fearsome reputation, and for a good reason. Not only are these natural born killers some of the deadliest predators in the insect world, they can also be deadly to people.

A killing frenzy

Asian giant hornets hunt other large insects, such as bees. In just a few hours, 30 or 40 hornets can wipe out an entire colony of 30,000 bees. They use their large jaws to cut the bees into shreds. The hornets are so efficient that each one can kill around 40 bees every minute. Once the killing spree is over, the hornets feed on the honey and bee larvae.

Location central and eastern Asia and parts of Russia

Adult size 50mm long

Number of species 1

The Asian giant hornet is the world's largest wasp. The deadly sting at the end of its tail is more than half a centimetre long.

KILLER INSECTS

Every year in Japan, more than 40 people die after being stung by the Asian giant hornet. This makes the insect Japan's number one deadliest creature.

27

Monarch butterfly

The Monarch butterfly lives in many different parts of the world, but it is very common in North America. These butterflies are easy to spot, because they are bright orange with black lines and cream spots along the tips of their wings. North American Monarch butterflies are found from southern Canada to Mexico. In summer they live in the north, then they fly south in the winter.

Filled with poison

Monarch **caterpillars** feed on poisonous plants called milkweeds. The poison builds up in the caterpillar's body. When the caterpillars change into butterflies, the poison is left in their bodies. Predators such as birds avoid eating the butterflies, because they taste so awful.

Location North America, Australia, South-east Asia, parts of western Europe

Adult size wingspan up to 10cm long

Number of species 1

MAJOR MIGRATION

During their **migration** from Canada to Mexico, some Monarch butterflies travel up to 3,000 kilometres.

A Monarch butterfly feeds on the **nectar** of a Mexican sunflower.

28

Vampire moth

Vampire moths are one of the few species of butterfly and moth that drink blood. They do this by sinking their sharp, tube-like mouthparts into the skin and drinking the blood. They prey on **mammals**, such as buffalo.

Location Europe and Asia

Adult size up to 1.5cm long

Number of species 17–19

A blood-sucking vampire moth rests on a twig. The dull brown colour of its body camouflages the moth from predators such as birds.

BLOOD SUCKERS

Vampire moths have been known to drink human blood. The bites can hurt, but these moths do not spread deadly diseases like other blood-sucking insects.

Evolution in action

One of the most important ideas in science is called evolution. It describes how living things gradually change over long periods of time to help them survive. Scientists think that the blood-sucking ability of vampire moths shows evolution in action. The relatives of vampire moths use their sharp mouthparts to pierce through fleshy fruits and eat their sweet juices. Animal skin is tougher than the skin of a fruit. Evolution has allowed the vampire moth to take advantage of a new source of food.

29

Blue damselfly

The beautiful blue damselfly is a common sight in Europe. Adults live near slow-moving rivers and ponds. They hunt small insects such as flies, ripping them apart with their strong jaws.

Location Europe

Adult size 30–35mm long

Number of species 1

Mating game

One of the oddest things about the blue damselfly is the way the males and females pair up to mate. The male clasps onto the female's neck, and the female bends her body around in an arc to meet him. This is called a mating wheel. After the pair have mated, the female flies over a pond or river and lays her eggs on a plant, just below the surface of the water. The eggs hatch into **nymphs**, which live in the water and hunt other small water animals, such as insect larvae.

Damselflies cannot walk! They fly everywhere and use their legs only to grasp onto objects when they land.

FREAKY FEATURE

Damselfly nymphs are fierce predators and grow very quickly. When the time comes, the nymphs climb a plant stem to get out of the water and **metamorphosize** into adult damselflies.

30

Flea

Fleas are wingless insects with sharp, tube-like mouthparts. They use them to pierce through the skin of animals and drink their blood. Different species prefer different animals, from cats and chickens to rats and people.

High jump!

Adult fleas do not have wings. Instead, they use their long back legs to jump onto their animal **hosts**. They find the animals by detecting the vibrations of their movement and the heat given off by their bodies. Fleas can jump great distances – up to 200 times their own body length. That's the same as a person jumping more than 330 metres from the spot.

Adult fleas must feed on the blood of their host before they can lay eggs and complete their life cycle.

Location worldwide

Adult size up to 3.3mm long

Number of species 2000

BLACK DEATH

Fleas can spread diseases. They were responsible for spreading the deadly bubonic plague, or Black Death. This disease killed millions of people in Europe during the **Middle Ages.**

31

Antlion

Antlions are the green stripy larvae of winged insects that look like dragonflies. They are predators. Some species have a cunning way of catching their prey. They dig shallow, funnel-shaped pits in the ground and lie in wait at the bottom. Small insects such as ants slip on the loose sand or soil and fall into the pit. The antlion then injects the insect with poison so it cannot move. It uses its sharp, pincer-like jaws to grab hold of its prey as it sucks the juices from its body. After the antlion has finished feeding, all that is left is the lifeless shell of its victim's body.

ANTLION ARTISTS

In North America, pit-digging antlions are known as 'doodlebugs' because they leave trails in the sand or soil that look like the doodles of an artist.

Location worldwide, except Antarctica

Adult size wingspan 2–15cm

Number of species 2000

Along with razor-sharp jaws, antlions have sharp claws. They use them to grip onto the stems and twigs they climb on.

Common earwig

The common earwig is a small insect with a pair of sharp pincers at the end of its tail. Earwigs get their name from a myth. These small insects often live in people's houses, and they are active at night. People once thought that earwigs crawled into people's ears at night and burrowed into their brains. In fact, earwigs are harmless. The worst an earwig will do is nip your skin with its pincers!

Location Europe, Asia and North Africa

Adult size up to 15mm long

Number of species 1

The pincers at the end of the earwig's body can deliver a painful pinch. The males use their pincers in fights over females.

CARING PARENTS

Female earwigs look after their eggs very carefully, and when the young hatch they watch over them for longer than other insects do.

Insect pests

Earwigs may be harmless, but they cause a lot of damage to the plants people grow as food. They will eat almost anything they can find, from cucumbers and cabbages to potatoes and pears. They are difficult to control, because they are active at night.

33

Cockroach

Cockroaches are one of the world's most common household **pests**. There are more than 4000 different species and they live in every continent apart from Antarctica. Most cockroaches are about the same size as a grape, but the world's biggest species – the aptly named giant cockroaches – can be up to 9 centimetres long. All cockroaches have small heads, flattened bodies and long, spiny legs. They rely on speed to escape from their enemies.

Scrap eaters

Only four or five cockroach species are pests. They shelter in the warmth of buildings such as hospitals and kitchens in our homes. Cockroaches are active at night, when they eat scraps of human food and other waste. They are dangerous because they carry the microscopic living things that cause diseases such as dysentery and polio.

Location worldwide

Adult size largest species is 9cm long

Number of species about 4500

The brown cockroach is a common pest. It hides away in cracks and crevices during the day and emerges at night to feed.

FREAKY FEATURE

Cockroaches will eat almost anything, from waste food to human hair and wallpaper. If no other food is available, they will even eat each other!

Weta

Location New Zealand

Adult size up to 10cm long

Number of species about 70

Wetas are a small group of insects from New Zealand. They live in many different places, from caves and forests to fields and gardens. These peculiar insects are some of the largest and heaviest in the world. The biggest species is the giant weta, which can be up to 10 centimetres long and weigh more than 40 grams.

Defence tactics

Wetas have several ways to protect themselves from their enemies. They have spines on their long back legs, which cause painful scratches. Then they have strong jaws, to deliver a painful bite. Some species hiss at their enemies as a warning call.

Some wetas play dead as a form of defence in the hope that predators will lose interest.

WHAT'S IN A NAME?

Maoris, the native people of New Zealand, call giant wetas by the name 'wetapunga', which means 'god of ugly things'.

Trapdoor spider

Location mainly tropical regions around the world

Adult size 1–5cm long

Number of species 120

Trapdoor spiders are amazing because they build clever burrows to help catch their prey. The burrow has a hinged lid that looks like the plug in a sink. When the unsuspecting prey passes by, the spider pushes the lid open, bursts out of its burrow, and – gotcha!

Building a burrow

Trapdoor spiders dig their burrows using rows of sharp teeth. They spin **silk** around mud and dead plants to form a plug to fill the hole. The spiders also spin silk around the inside of the burrow. Fine silk threads lead from the burrow to the outside, so the spiders can 'feel' when prey may be passing overhead.

FREAKY FEATURE

Female trapdoor spiders spend almost all their lives underground. Some species can live as long as 20 years!

Trapdoor spiders have strong jaws and sharp **fangs** that they use to stab their prey.

Fat-tailed scorpion

The fat-tailed scorpion is the most dangerous scorpion in the world. The sting at the end of its fat tail delivers a powerful poison that spreads from the wound into the body. Anyone who is unlucky enough to be stung will quickly start to feel very ill. The sting is incredibly painful, and it also causes other effects, such as chest pain, sickness, blurred vision and even death.

Tail attack

The fat-tailed scorpion uses its sting mainly to attack and kill insects and small mammals for food. It uses its front pincers to pin down its victim, before it arches its fat tail over and stabs it. The poison quickly takes effect, and the deadly scorpion devours its meal.

POPULAR PETS

Amazingly, some people keep fat-tailed scorpions as pets. Try not to pick one up, though!

Location deserts in Africa and the Middle East

Adult size up to 10cm long

Number of species about 18

The sting of the deadly fat-tailed scorpion can kill a person in less than two hours! The venom is stored in glands in the tail.

Ogre-faced spider

Ogre-faced spiders are huge, with long, slender legs. They get their name because they have long fangs and massive eyes, which make them look like ogres. They are nocturnal, which means they are active at night.

Casting a net

Ogre-faced spiders are also known as net-casting spiders. They spin their webs into nets between their front legs, then throw them at their prey such as beetles, moths, flies and sometimes other spiders. The nets are stretchy and sticky, to trap their prey. The spider then delivers a poisonous bite to stop its victim from moving. If the spider does not catch a meal, it eats its web and spins a new one the next night.

Location tropical regions across the world

Adult size female up to 2.5cm long

Number of species 57

FREAKY FEATURE

The ogre-faced spider's large eyes give it excellent eyesight at night, for throwing the net over its victim.

The ogre-faced spider actually has eight eyes! Six smaller eyes are dwarfed by the two huge eyes on the spider's head, making it appear to be two-eyed only.

Jumping spider

Jumping spiders are the largest group of spiders, with more than 5000 species. As you can guess from their name, these spiders move by jumping from place to place. Most jumping spiders are small, with short legs and an unusual pattern of eyes on their head. They have four large eyes on their face and four smaller eyes on top of their head. Jumping spiders use their excellent eyesight to keep a lookout for insect prey.

Hunting prey

Unlike most spiders, jumping spiders do not use webs to trap their food. Instead, they creep up on their victims, then pounce on them like a cat. They can jump more than 50 times the length of their own body. Before making a jump, the spider spins a line of silk and fixes it to the ground. This acts like a climber's safety rope, anchoring the spider in case it falls.

Jumping spiders are active during the day. They use their many eyes to spot and stalk prey before pouncing on their victim.

Location mostly tropical regions around the world

Adult size varies according to species

Number of species 5000

Crab spider

Crab spiders have flat bodies and two long pairs of front legs that look like the pincers and legs of a crab. Crab spiders are ambush hunters – they lie in wait for passing insect prey. They rely on camouflage to hide in their surroundings.

Master of disguise

The bird-dung crab spider takes its disguise one step further. The bodies of these dark brown spiders are covered in bumps and warts, making them look like bird poo. To add to the effect, the spiders also spin small threads of fine, white silk that look like the white bits of the bird poo.

Location Asia, from Indonesia to Japan

Adult size around 15mm long

Number of species about 2000

FREAKY FEATURE

Not only does the bird-dung crab spider look like bird poo, it even smells like it! The smell attracts prey such as small insects, but puts off predators such as birds.

Crab spiders do not build webs to catch prey. Instead they blend in with leaves and flowers and grab insects using their front legs.

Spiny-backed spider

The spiny-backed spider is an arachnid with a swollen, spiny body. It is named after the black spines on the end of its body, but only the females have these spines. The males are much smaller, with flat bodies.

Spinning a line

Spiny-backed spiders live in the treetops and build spiral-shaped webs to trap flying insects. Again, only the female spiders build these amazing webs. The male uses his silk to weave a mating thread to the female's web. Then he runs out and mates with the female.

Location North and Central America

Adult size females up to 12mm long

Number of species about 70

Spine

The sharp spines on the back of this spiny-backed spider protect it from predators such as birds.

FREAKY FEATURE

Male spiny-backed spiders beware! After mating, they must escape quickly or they might be eaten by the females.

Camel spider

Camel spiders do not look like most spiders, but they are arachnids. Like other arachnids, they have two body parts, eight legs and pincer-like mouthparts. Most hunt termites, beetles and other insects, but the largest species will eat larger animals, such as snakes, lizards and mice. Camel spiders use their powerful mouthparts to cut their prey into pieces. Then they squirt saliva on the body parts, turning them into liquid food.

The fear factor

There are many tall stories about camel spiders. They are big, but they are not the biggest arachnids. Camel spiders are also fast runners, but they are not as fast as many people think.

SPIDER MYTHS

Some people in Arab countries think that camel spiders eat human flesh. This is not true. Camel spider bites, though painful, are very rare.

Camel spiders are also known as screaming spiders because of the noise they make when they chase after their prey.

Location warm regions around the world, except Australia

Adult size up to 7cm long

Number of species about 1000

Dust mite

Dust mites are so small that they are invisible to the human eye. But these tiny creatures live by their millions in our houses and homes. Beds, carpets and furniture are popular places for dust mites because there is plenty of food – flakes of dead human skin and hair.

Chemical reaction

Most people do not know they are living with dust mites because they cannot see them. But some people cannot stand these tiny creatures. That's because they suffer from a reaction to the dust mite's droppings, which contain chemicals that cause illnesses such as **asthma** and **eczema**.

Location worldwide

Adult size 0.4 mm long

Number of species 3

WHAT'S IN A NAME?

Dust mites are often called 'bed bugs' because they live in beds. But bed bugs are a different type of creepy crawly — they are insects. Dust mites are arachnids — close relatives of scorpions and spiders.

Scientists estimate that the pillows and mattress of a typical bed can house up to 6 billion dust mites!

43

Quiz

Now you have read about some of the world's most extraordinary bugs, try this fun quiz to see how much you remember. All the answers can be found in the pages of this book. (You can also find them on page 48.)

Cicada

1. Which of these insects causes the deadly Chagas disease?
a) cockroach
b) bombardier beetle
c) thorn bug   d) assassin bug

2. Dung beetles were worshipped by which ancient people?
a) Greeks   b) Romans
c) Egyptians   d) Aztecs

3. How many legs does an insect have?
a) 3   b) 2   c) 5   d) 6

4. What is the name of the world's heaviest insect?
a) Goliath beetle   b) cicada
c) honey bee   d) leaf insect

5. What is the name of the world's longest insect?
a) leaf insect   b) Hercules beetle
c) Borneo stick insect   d) flea

6. What do we call the middle part of an insect's body?
a) abdomen   b) thorax
c) trunk   d) antenna

7. What do we call the larva of a butterfly?
a) mite   b) caterpillar
c) nymph   d) maggot

8. Which insect spreads the deadly disease malaria?
a) robber fly   b) mosquito
c) giant water bug   d) bullet ant

9. Which insect can jump more than 200 times its own body length?
a) army ant   b) flea
c) weta   d) cockroach

10. Which of these creepy crawlies does not use poison to kill its prey?
a) scorpion b) antlion
c) Monarch butterfly d) flea

11. Which insect is known for its long migration?
a) hornet b) bee
c) Monarch butterfly d) army ant

12. Which animal has a deadly sting in its tail?
a) trapdoor spider b) antlion
c) earwig d) scorpion

13. Which of these creepy crawlies looks and smells like bird poo?
a) spiny-backed spider b) flea
c) ant-decapitating fly
d) bird-dung crab spider

14. What do we call the substance that most spiders spin to build their webs?
a) cotton b) silk
c) wool d) linen

15. Which of the following animals is not an arachnid?
a) spiny-backed spider
b) fat-tailed scorpion c) weta
d) trapdoor spider

16. How many legs does a spider have?
a) 4 b) 6 c) 8 d) 10

17. Which of these spiders does not spin a web of silk to catch its prey?
a) spiny-backed spider
b) jumping spider
c) trapdoor spider
d) ogre-faced spider

18. What do we call the larva of a fly?
a) maggot b) mite
c) caterpillar d) nymph

19. What is the name of the world's strongest insect?
a) Hercules beetle b) hornet
c) assassin bug d) mosquito

20. Which of these insects does not feed on human blood?
a) mosquito b) vampire moth
c) flea d) damselfly

Monarch butterfly

Glossary

abdomen the end part of the body of an insect or arachnid

arachnids one of a group of insects with eight legs, including mites, scorpions and spiders

asthma a condition in which breathing is difficult

blisters swellings on the skin

burrow a hole underground dug by an animal, or to dig into the soil

camouflage colours and marks on an animal that help it to blend in with its surroundings

cannibalism when an animal eats another animal of its own species

carbon dioxide a gas present in the air

caterpillars the larvae of a butterfly or moth

colony a group of animals living together

compound eyes eyes made up of hundreds of tiny units

decapitating cutting the head off something

dung the poo of animals that eat plants

eczema a condition in which skin is dry and sore

eyespots eye-like markings on an insect designed to scare away predators

fangs long, sharp teeth

hatch when young break out of an egg

hosts animals that support another animal

larvae the tiny worm-like young of some insects

life cycle changes an animal goes through from birth to death

malaria a disease that can result in death. People are infected with malaria when they are bitten by a mosquito.

mammals animals with fur that feed their young with milk

mate to breed to make babies

metamorphosize to change from a larva to an adult

microscopic too small to be seen by the eye, to be viewed using a microscope

Middle Ages period in history from about AD 1100 to 1500

migration the long journey some animals make to find a new place to live

moulting shedding the skin

nectar the sugary liquid produced by flowers

nymphs the young forms of insects

parasites animals that live on or inside another animal

permanent lasting for ever or a long time

pests animals that eat our food crops or live in our homes

predators animals that hunt other animals

prey an animal that is hunted by other animals

rainforests thick forest habitats where it is warm and wet

sacs parts of an animal that are shaped like a bag

saliva juices produced in the mouth that help to break down food

sap the juices that run through the stems of plants

sense the way animals detect things, for example eyesight or hearing

silk the long thread produced by spiders to make webs

snout the long nose of an animal

species animals of the same type that can breed and make babies

symbol something that is used to represent or suggest something

temporary existing only for a short time, not permanent

thorax the middle part of an insect's body

tropical hot regions around the Equator

vibrate move a small distance backwards and forwards very rapidly

warts small, hard lumps on skin

Further information

Books

Bomb-factory Beetles and Other Weird Insects by Carmen Bredeson (Enslow, 2009)

Buzz (Dorling Kindersley, 2007)

What's That Bug?: Everyday Insects and Their Really Cool Cousins by Nan Froman (Madison Press Books, 2010)

Bugs by Terry Jennings (QED Publishing, 2009)

Bugs Pop-up: Creepy Crawlers Face-to-Face by Sally Hewitt (Harry N. Abrams, 2010)

Kingdom: Micro Monsters (Kingfisher, 2010)

Insects: Biggest! Littlest! by Sandra Markle (Boyds Mills Press, 2009)

Bugs on Your Body: Nature's Creepiest Creatures Live on You! by John Perritano (Gareth Stevens Publishing, 2009)

Websites

Discover everything you need to know about the insect world:

www.earthlife.net/insects

Learn about all sorts of different creepy crawlies at the website of the Natural History Museum, London:

www.nhm.ac.uk/nature-online/life/insects-spiders

Meet some more weird and wonderful insects at:

www.insecta-inspecta.com

Weta

Index

Quiz answers: 1 d   2 c   3 d   4 a   5 c   6 b   7 b   8 b   9 b   10 c   11 c
12 d   13 d   14 b   15 c   16 c   17 b and c   18 a   19 a   20 d